CHESTER ARTHUR

The Presidents of the United States

George Washington
1789–1797

John Adams
1797–1801

Thomas Jefferson
1801–1809

James Madison
1809–1817

James Monroe
1817–1825

John Quincy Adams
1825–1829

Andrew Jackson
1829–1837

Martin Van Buren
1837–1841

William Henry Harrison
1841

John Tyler
1841–1845

James Polk
1845–1849

Zachary Taylor
1849–1850

Millard Fillmore
1850–1853

Franklin Pierce
1853–1857

James Buchanan
1857–1861

Abraham Lincoln
1861–1865

Andrew Johnson
1865–1869

Ulysses S. Grant
1869–1877

Rutherford B. Hayes
1877–1881

James Garfield
1881

Chester Arthur
1881–1885

Grover Cleveland
1885–1889

Benjamin Harrison
1889–1893

Grover Cleveland
1893–1897

William McKinley
1897–1901

Theodore Roosevelt
1901–1909

William H. Taft
1909–1913

Woodrow Wilson
1913–1921

Warren Harding
1921–1923

Calvin Coolidge
1923–1929

Herbert Hoover
1929–1933

Franklin D. Roosevelt
1933–1945

Harry Truman
1945–1953

Dwight Eisenhower
1953–1961

John F. Kennedy
1961–1963

Lyndon B. Johnson
1963–1969

Richard Nixon
1969–1974

Gerald Ford
1974–1977

Jimmy Carter
1977–1981

Ronald Reagan
1981–1989

George H. W. Bush
1989–1993

William J. Clinton
1993–2001

George W. Bush
2001–2009

Barack Obama
2009–

CHESTER ARTHUR

STEVEN OTFINOSKI

 **Marshall Cavendish**
Benchmark
New York

Marshall Cavendish Benchmark
99 White Plains Road
Tarrytown, NY 10591-5502
www.marshallcavendish.us

All Internet addresses were correct at the time of printing.

Library of Congress Cataloging-in-Publication Data

Otfinoski, Steven.
Chester Arthur / by Steven Otfinoski.
p. cm. — (Presidents and their times)
Summary: "Provides comprehensive information on President Chester Arthur and places him within his historical and cultural context. Also explored are the formative events of his times and how he responded"—Provided by publisher.
Includes bibliographical references and index.
ISBN 978-0-7614-3625-6
1. Arthur, Chester Alan, 1829–1886—Juvenile literature. 2. Presidents—United States—Biography—Juvenile literature. I. Title.
E692.O86 2010
973.8'4092—dc22
[B]
2008010253

Editor: Christine Florie
Publisher: Michelle Bisson
Art Director: Anahid Hamparian
Series Designer: Alex Ferrari

Photo research by Connie Gardner

Cover photo by National Portrait Gallery/Art Resource

The photographs in this book are used by permission and through the courtesy of: *Bridgeman Art Library:* President Chester A. Arthur (colour litho) Huntington, Daniel (1816–1906) (after)/Private Collection, Peter Newark American Pictures, 3, 95, 97(R); Easter Eggs In Town (colour/litho) Terre Charles Henry (1864–1926)/Musee de la ville de Paris, France Archives, Charmet; 46; *NorthWind Picture Archives:* 6, 36; *Corbis:* James P. Blair, 9; Corbis, 20, 30, 40, 58, 97(L); Bettmann, 24, 28, 34, 42, 50, 83; *The Image Works:* Mary Evans Picture Library, 62; *The Granger Collection:* 10, 16, 17, 18, 22, 33, 49, 54, 61, 66, 68, 76, 77, 79, 80; *Alamy:* NorthWind Picture Archives, 13, 69, 96 (L); *Digital Railroad:* Darlene Bordwell, 14; *Art Resource:* New York Public Library, 26, 65, 88; *Getty Images:* Hulton Archive, 37, 45, 74, 86, 91, 96 (R); *Art Archive:* Culver Pictures, 53.

Printed in Malaysia
1 3 5 6 4 2

CONTENTS

★ ★ ★ ★ ★ ★ ★ ★ ★ ★ ★ ★ ★ ★ ★ ★ ★ ★ ★

After the assassination of President James Garfield, Vice President Chester Arthur took the oath of office, in 1881.

A PREACHER'S SON One

*I*t had been a long ten weeks for Vice President Chester Arthur, the longest summer of his life. On July 2, 1881, President James A. Garfield had been shot by a disgruntled office seeker at a Washington, D.C., train station. At first it looked as if Garfield would recover, but as the days wore into weeks and the weeks into months, the president's condition worsened.

The country and the government came to a standstill that terrible summer. As the vice president, Arthur might have been expected to take on presidential duties, but because Garfield was still alive, that seemed to Arthur presumptuous. Besides, Arthur had other reasons for keeping a low profile during the president's recuperation. The madman who had shot Garfield, Charles Guiteau, had declared boldly as he was arrested that now "Arthur will be President." Only Arthur's worst enemies actually believed that Arthur and his supporters, conservative Republicans who called themselves **Stalwarts**, were implicated in Garfield's shooting, but the statement cast a shadow over the vice president's already dubious reputation.

The fact was, few Americans wanted to see Chester Arthur become president. He had never served in elected office before and had been chosen by the party leaders for the office of vice president only because he represented the Stalwarts and therefore balanced out the Republican ticket. Arthur's character was in as much doubt as his experience. The former president Rutherford B. Hayes had fired Arthur from his position as collector of the

Custom House of the Port of New York, a center of corruption. Arthur personally had not been accused of corruption, but at the very least he had allowed it to flourish all around him. How could such a man be trusted as president?

On September 19, 1881, the news spread across the country that Garfield, after a long, valiant fight, was dying. Later that evening the grim news that the president was dead reached Arthur at his home in New York City. Reporters flocked to Arthur's Manhattan townhouse to get a statement, but his doorman, Alec Powell, would not let them in. "I dare not disturb him," he told the reporters. Arthur was indeed in no condition to receive them. The man about to become the twenty-first president of the United States was sitting alone in a room, crying like a baby, his head buried in his hands. He was crying for Garfield, but he was also crying for himself. He had never wanted to be president. Chester Arthur was satisfied with the wealth and influence he had already achieved. He felt unprepared for this, the greatest challenge of his life.

Family Background

Chester Alan Arthur was born on October 5, 1829, in a log cabin in the small farming community of Fairfield, Vermont, in the state's northwest corner. He was named after Dr. Chester Abell, the physician and close family friend who delivered him. He received his middle name from his grandfather, Alan Arthur. When told of his son's birth, William Arthur, it is said, danced joyfully. This might have seemed a strange reaction for a Baptist minister, but the Arthurs had prayed fervently for a son after having four daughters, and Elder Arthur, as his congregants addressed him, was anything but a typical clergyman.

Chester Arthur was born in 1829 in Fairfield, Vermont. This is a reconstruction of his birthplace.

William Arthur, who was of Scotch-Irish descent, was born in County Antrim in northern Ireland in 1796. In about 1818 he emigrated from Ireland, where he had few job prospects, to Quebec, Canada. He taught school in Dunham, 15 miles north of the Vermont border. He married the eighteen-year-old Malvina

Arthur's father, William, was an ordained minister known for his fiery sermons.

Stone, Arthur's mother, in 1821. The Stone family was of English descent and had lived in New Hampshire since 1763. Malvina's grandfather Uriah had fought in the Continental Army during the American Revolution. His son George Washington Stone moved to Berkshire, Vermont, to farm in about 1800. He married a Vermonter, Judith Stevens, and Malvina, their first child, was born in 1802.

In 1827 William Arthur attended a revival meeting in Burlington, Vermont, and converted to the Free Will Baptist Church. He was ordained as a minister in the denomination the following May. Soon after, William was called to lead a congregation in Fairfield, to which the family moved. Elder Arthur's salary was a meager one, and he supplemented his income by teaching school and preaching at other churches throughout Vermont and Canada.

William Arthur's sermons were eloquent but hard-edged. He was an **abolitionist**, a person opposed to slavery at a time when it was still an accepted institution. Even in New England, where slavery had largely been banned, abolitionists were looked on by many as troublemakers and rabble-rousers.

"Reverend William Arthur was a man of ability and originality of character, who formed his opinions without much reference to the views of others, and was most persistent and vigorous in asserting and maintaining them," a friend said of him. Fiery sermons on abolition were poorly tolerated by Elder Arthur's Fairfield congregation, and he was soon asked to leave. He and his family moved on to find another congregation. By the time young Chester, known as Chet, was ten, the family had moved five times. In November 1839 they settled in Union Village, New York (now the town of Greenwich), where the boy attended the local academy. Before that his father had taught him at home.

STUDENT AND TEACHER

In 1844, when Chester was fifteen years old, the family moved to Schenectady, New York, where the tall, handsome youth went to the Lyceum, a preparatory school for nearby Union College. "His eyes were dark and brilliant, and his physical system finely formed," one teacher recalled of young Chet. "He was frank and open in his manners, and genial in his disposition." A fairly good student known for his quick mind, Arthur coedited *The Lyceum Review*, the school newspaper. He also displayed his developing interest in politics.

A fervent supporter of the **Whig Party** presidential candidate Henry Clay, Arthur got himself into a fight with several classmates who opposed Clay. "I have been in many a political battle since then," Arthur remembered years later, "but none livelier, or that more thoroughly enlisted me."

In September 1845 he was accepted into the sophomore class of Union College, thanks to his advanced studies at the Lyceum. His family had little money to give him for college, so Arthur worked during school vacations as a teacher to pay for his schooling. At Union he was selected for the academic fraternity Phi Beta Kappa. He also served as president of the debating society. "In disposition he was genial and very sociable," a classmate later recalled, "and he had a good relative standing in his class though not a very diligent student."

The eighteen-year-old Arthur graduated in July 1848 in the top third of his class. He moved to Schaghticoke, New York, where he worked full-time at teaching. He left within a year and studied law briefly at the new State and National Law School in Ballston Spa, New York. Several months later, unable to continue paying for his studies, Arthur returned home to his family in Hoosick, New York. In 1851 his father helped him secure a position as principal and teacher of an academy in North Pownal, Vermont. Classes were held in the basement of the church where Elder Arthur preached. Although an effective teacher, the future president saw teaching primarily as a way to earn money so that he could pursue his real ambition—to become a lawyer.

In November 1852 Arthur was hired as principal of an academy in Cohoes, New York, where his sister Malvina taught. It would be his last teaching position. The following year he moved to New York City to find a job in the legal profession.

To help pay for his education at Union College, Arthur worked as a teacher.

UNION COLLEGE

One of the oldest liberal arts colleges in New York State, Union College opened its doors in 1779 but was not officially chartered until 1795. It was the first college chartered by the Board of Regents of the State of New York. Besides President Chester Arthur, its two most distinguished political alumni are William H. Seward and Robert Toombs. By a strange twist of fate, both men served as secretary of state at the same time—Seward for the Union and Toombs for the Confederacy during the Civil War.

Civil Rights Lawyer

Arthur was hired in March 1853 as law clerk in the office of Erastus D. Culver, a leading abolitionist attorney his family had known back in Union Village. In those days many young men could not afford to attend law school and prepared for the profession by working as law clerks and studying in their spare time. A fast learner, Arthur was admitted to the bar the following year, in May 1854. Culver hired him as a partner in his practice, changing the firm's name to Culver, Parker, and Arthur. The firm took on a number of cases defending freed blacks and slaves from persecution. Arthur, as ardent an abolitionist as his father, was involved in a number of these cases.

One of the most significant civil rights cases that Arthur and his firm handled concerned eight slaves owned by Jonathon Lemmon. Lemmon and his wife had brought the slaves to New York City by boat from Virginia in 1852 and were preparing to transport them to Texas. Louis Napoleon, a free black man, found out about these plans and obtained a court order that declared the slaves to be freemen. New York State law said that no person could be held in bondage. Lemmon refused to accept this, claiming that his slaves were not New York residents but merely passing through on their way to Texas, a state where slavery was legal. Arthur's firm defended the slaves and won three judgments in their favor, the last in 1860, before the New York Court of Appeals. The eight slaves were legally freed.

In the most celebrated civil rights case that Arthur personally tried, he defended a black public school teacher, Elizabeth Jennings. On July 16, 1854, Jennings sat in a whites-only Brooklyn streetcar. When the conductor told her to move, she refused.

ONE SCHOOL, TWO FUTURE PRESIDENTS

Three years after Arthur left North Pownal Academy, a student at Williams College in Massachusetts came to the academy to teach penmanship. His name was James A. Garfield. Garfield taught at the school for the winter, while still attending college. Unlike Arthur, he saw teaching as a promising career. After graduating from Williams, Garfield was appointed professor of Latin and Greek at Western Reserve Eclectic Institute (later Hiram College) in his home state of Ohio. Within a year, at the age of twenty-six, he was named the school's president. But politics eventually drew Garfield's interest. He was elected a member of the Ohio state senate in 1859.

Twenty-one years later, Garfield and Arthur would share the Republican presidential ticket. These two former teachers at the North Pownal Academy would in turn become the twentieth and twenty-first presidents of the United States.

In 1853 Arthur obtained a position as a law clerk for a New York City firm that took on many cases that defended African Americans.

The conductor then physically threw her off the streetcar. Arthur took on the case, arguing that such segregation on a public transportation vehicle was illegal. He referred to a section of a statute that read "colored persons, if sober, well-behaved, and free from

Before Arthur's 1854 case defending Elizabeth Jennings, street cars in New York City were segregated.

disease" could not be arbitrarily expelled from a common carrier. Arthur won, and Jennings was awarded $250 in damages. More important, the New York State Court moved that all state public transportation from then on would be integrated.

Politics and Romance

Arthur's strong abolitionist beliefs soon brought him into politics. The Whig Party he had supported disbanded in 1852, and two years later a new political organization, the **Republican Party**, was born. The party's platform rested on a strong stand against slavery, with emphasis on banning the practice in the new territories, such as Kansas. Arthur became one of the founding fathers of the New York Republican Party. In 1856 the first Republican presidential convention, held in Philadelphia, nominated the explorer and soldier John Frémont for the presidency. Frémont would go on to lose the election that fall to the Democrat James Buchanan.

Two other major events in Arthur's life occurred that same year. He met Ellen (Nell) Herndon, the attractive nineteen-year-old daughter of the naval officer William Lewis Herndon. The two fell in love and were soon engaged. He also opened his own law practice with his friend Henry D. Gardiner. The two young lawyers traveled to the territory of Kansas. Arthur and Gardiner were among many enterprising men eager to accept the government's offer of cheap land there. But Kansas was not a peaceful place to do business. The Kansas-Nebraska Act, passed by Congress in 1854, declared that residents of those two territories could vote to decide whether they would enter the Union as free states or states in which slavery was allowed.

Ellen Lewis Herndon married Chester Arthur on October 25, 1859.

"Bleeding Kansas"

The territory of Kansas earned its terrible nickname after the Kansas-Nebraska Act of 1854 was passed. Settlers on both sides of the issue set up their own communities as tensions rose. On May 21, 1856, proslavery "Border Ruffians" from Missouri raided Lawrence, Kansas, an abolitionist stronghold. Four days later John Brown, a fanatical abolitionist who had relocated to Kansas, led a raiding party that included four of his sons along Pottawatomie Creek to avenge the Lawrence raid. Entering a proslavery settlement in the early-morning hours, they hacked five unarmed men to death with broadswords. The bloodshed then spread across the territory, and by the year's end some two hundred people on both sides were dead.

After a less violent legislative struggle between the two groups, in 1859 state lawmakers passed a constitution that included a provision forbidding slavery. But the earlier bloodshed over slavery would prove to be prophetic. Kansas was admitted to the Union as the thirty-fourth state in January 1861; two and half months later the Civil War began.

Both proslavery and antislavery settlers poured into Kansas, each faction hoping to gain a majority when the territory voted on the issue. The two sides often clashed in violent confrontations. While wanting to help make Kansas free of slavery, Arthur was shocked by the bloody violence, and he decided to return to New York, to fight against slavery more peacefully, within the

Proslave and antislave settlers clash over the Kansas-Nebraska Act.

legal system. He had another urgent reason to head back east. Ellen's father had died in a shipwreck during a storm off Cape Hatteras, North Carolina. The brave captain had gone down with the ship, having evacuated the women and children passengers.

Herndon then proceeded to keep order on board the sinking ship and refused to leave his post. His courageous actions were soon immortalized in a monument to him erected at the United States Naval Academy in Annapolis, Maryland.

Arthur returned immediately to New York City to be with the grieving Nell. He took over the legal and financial responsibility for the Herndon family. The city would remain his home base for the rest of his life.

A political cartoon by Thomas Nast satirizes President Andrew Jackson and the spoils system that originated during his administration.

GENTLEMAN BOSS Two

After a long engagement, Chester Arthur and Nell Herndon were married on October 25, 1859, in Calvary Episcopal Church on Fourth Avenue in New York City. The newlyweds moved into Nell's mother's townhouse on West Twenty-first Street, south of Madison Square Park. The ambitious Arthur plunged into state politics. He worked hard during the reelection campaign of the Republican New York governor Edwin D. Morgan in 1860. Arthur's efforts caught the attention of the New York political boss Thurlow Weed, who recommended the young man to Governor Morgan. In his next term Morgan appointed Arthur to the post of state engineer-in-chief. The position was largely ceremonial and had little to do with engineering. Arthur was a member of the governor's staff and attended ceremonies with Morgan on state occasions.

THE SPOILS SYSTEM

Arthur's appointment was a classic example of the **spoils system** at work. This system of political payback had been around in government since the days of President Andrew Jackson. It was based on the old adage "To the victor go the spoils." In political life this meant that a loyal party worker could expect to be rewarded with a job when his candidate got into office, regardless of whether he was qualified for the position. The officeholder was then expected to pay back his benefactor by handing over to the party treasury a percentage of his salary. Thurlow Weed, Arthur's first mentor, oversaw the spoils system in New York State and within the next decade would guide it to its peak of influence.

THURLOW WEED

During his long public career Thurlow Weed was an influential journalist, editor, and political boss. He also had a hand in the formation of three important political parties. He was born in Greene County, New York, in 1797. A self-made man, Weed started as an apprentice printer and rose

to be publisher of the *Rochester Telegraph* when he was only twenty-eight years old. In 1826 he helped form the nation's first political third party, the Anti-Masonic Party. Soon afterward he abandoned the new group for the Whig Party and, as editor of the *Albany Evening Journal*, was its main spokesperson for more than two decades. Weed helped win the presidential nomination for several Whig candidates, including Arthur's first political hero, Henry Clay, in 1832 and 1844.

By 1860 Weed was a Republican and had managed the unsuccessful presidential nomination campaign of William H. Seward. Abraham Lincoln beat Seward for the nomination and went on to become president. Weed served as an adviser to Lincoln during the Civil War and was sent to Europe as a special agent for the Union. After Lincoln's death, Weed supported Lincoln's successor, Andrew Johnson. But Johnson's failed policies and impeachment by the Radical Republicans ended Weed's time in the national spotlight. He moved to New York City in 1867, where he played a key role in Republican politics until his death, in 1882.

Many of the political appointees given jobs under the spoils system were unqualified and exerted little effort. This was not the case with Chester Arthur. He was an energetic worker and an able administrator. He would soon have the opportunity to prove himself worthy of greater responsibility.

THE CIVIL WAR

In the same national election that returned Edwin Morgan to the New York governorship, the Republicans elected their first president, Abraham Lincoln of Illinois. Lincoln, like many Northerners, was not an abolitionist. Although he did not want slavery to spread to the new territories, he was willing to allow the practice to continue where it already existed. His election, however, was seen as an affront by many residents of the South. They feared that the new president, who believed strongly in the power of the federal government, would threaten their states' rights and attempt to end slavery in the South at that time. Slavery was essential to the

Secessionists unfurl the first state's rights flag at the capitol in South Carolina.

economy of the South at that time, which was based on agriculture. Unpaid labor kept Southern farms and plantations profitable. Within a month of Lincoln's inauguration, Southern states began **seceding**, or withdrawing, from the Union. They formed their own political entity, the Confederate States of America. Lincoln, who had declared secession illegal in his inaugural address, warned the rebel states, known as the Confederacy, that he would hold and protect federal forts in the South. On April 12, 1861, Confederate troops fired on the federal Fort Sumter in Charleston Harbor, South Carolina, and forced its surrender. The Civil War had begun.

Governor Morgan appointed Arthur as assistant **quartermaster** general for New York. The quartermaster's job was to obtain supplies, food, shelter, and clothing for the flood of volunteers for the Union army streaming into New York City from all over the Northeast. His organizational and administrative skills made Arthur the perfect choice for this position. He used tact and diplomacy in smoothing over the conflicts that arose between the sometimes raucous soldiers and the residents of New York. He lowered costs by contracting with the lowest bidders in private business for food and supplies, instead of having the government prepare the food and goods. He personally inspected all supplies bought by his department, making sure they were of the highest quality. One aide described Arthur as "industrious, energetic and watchful" and said the assistant quartermaster "appeared to like his official duties." Arthur did such an outstanding job that in February 1862 the governor promoted him to inspector general and five months later made him quartermaster general. Arthur conducted the government's business with complete honesty. He had plenty of opportunities to "skim," or take for himself some of the money designated for contractors, but he never did so.

As the bloody war dragged on, many Northerners wanted the government to make peace with the South and allow the Southern Confederacy to coexist with the Union. Lincoln refused to consider this. He would not allow the United States to split into

The office in which Chester Arthur worked as the assistant quartermaster in New York is pictured here.

two separate nations. This stand proved unpopular, and the Republicans lost much of their public support. In the 1862 gubernatorial elections in New York, Morgan was defeated by the Democrat Horatio Seymour. The new governor put his own men into top state offices, and Arthur lost his position as quartermaster general. His successor, General S. V. Talcott, had only high praise for Arthur. "[H]is practical good sense and unremitting exertion," wrote Talcott, "at a period when everything was in confusion, reduced the operations of this department to a matured plan, by which large amounts of money were saved to the . . . government."

A Death in the Family

Arthur returned to his law practice and prospered. Then personal tragedy struck. On July 8, 1863, three-year-old William, the Arthurs' first child, died suddenly of what the doctors called an "affection" of the brain. Actually, he suffered an infection that inflamed his brain.

"We have lost our darling boy," the grief-stricken Arthur wrote his brother. "It came upon us so unexpectedly and suddenly. Nell is broken hearted. I fear much for her health. You know how her heart was wrapped up in her dear boy." The couple felt an unreasonable guilt over their son's death, fearing that they had taxed his young mind too much. When their second child, Alan Jr., was born in 1864, they would go out of their way to spoil him. Seven years later their daughter Ellen was born.

As the Union army went from defeats to victories against the South, the fortunes of the Republican Party improved, and Lincoln won reelection in 1864. The Civil War finally ended in the Union victory in April 1865. Without inherited money or family connections, Arthur looked to politics once more as a way to increase his future list of legal clients.

Reconstruction

Five days after the Confederate commander General Robert E. Lee surrendered to the Union general Ulysses S. Grant at the Appomattox Court House in Virginia, President Lincoln was assassinated by the Southern sympathizer John Wilkes Booth while watching a play at Ford's Theater in Washington, D.C. Vice President Andrew Johnson, who then became president, was a former senator from Tennessee. A Southerner who had remained loyal to the Union, Johnson tried to carry out Lincoln's plans to bring the Confederate states back into the Union as quickly and painlessly as possible. But the **Radical Republicans** wanted to punish the South during this postwar period, known as the **Reconstruction**. They opposed Johnson's plans to rebuild the South, imposed military rule, took civil liberties from former Confederate officials such as the right to vote, and gave **suffrage** and other rights to freed blacks.

Among the most powerful and flamboyant Republicans of the Reconstruction period was Roscoe Conkling of New York, who was elected to the U.S. Senate in 1867. Conkling supported the former Union general Ulysses S. Grant for president. Conkling and other conservative Republicans also supported the spoils system, which continued to flourish during the postwar period.

Arthur was drawn to Conkling and his power. Soon the senator became Arthur's mentor, although the two men were the same age. Together they worked tirelessly, campaigning for Grant's presidential nomination and then his election in 1868. Grant, a great military leader who had little experience with politics, rewarded Senator Conkling by giving him the right to make all federal appointments in New York, the most populous state at that time. One of Conkling's first decisions was to make his chief lieutenant, Chester Arthur, a counsel to the state tax commission at a salary of $10,000 a year.

A proud, willful man, Conkling made no apologies for the political system he presided over in New York. "We are told that the

Freemen of the South vote during the period known as Reconstruction.

Republican Party is a machine," he said (a machine in this context being a small group of men who controlled a political organization). "Yes. A government is a machine. . . . Every organization which binds men together for a common cause is a machine."

LORD ROSCOE

Roscoe Conkling's thirst for power made him for a time one of the most influential senators in the nation, but it also brought about his precipitous downfall.

The son of a federal judge who had also served in Congress, Conkling was born in Albany, New York, on October 30, 1829. He studied law and was admitted to the bar in 1850. That same year he was appointed, at age  twenty-one, district attorney for Oneida County. Conkling was elected to the U.S. House of Representatives in 1859 and served until 1863. He again served in the House from 1865 to 1867, when he was elected to the Senate. For nearly a decade Conkling, dubbed "Lord Roscoe" by his enemies, controlled all federal appointments in New York State. He was a tall, handsome man with a hot temper. Strong and athletic, Conkling was an amateur boxer who trained in his own private gym.

When the Ohio Republican governor Rutherford B. Hayes, a reformer, was elected president, Conkling's spoils system came under fierce attack. Conkling's attempt to bring Grant back into the White House in 1880 failed, and James Garfield, another reform Republican, was elected president. Conkling resigned his Senate seat in protest of Garfield's efforts to end the spoils system in New York. He expected the voters to reelect him to his seat, but people were tired of Lord Roscoe. Conkling returned to his law practice and never won public office again.

He was walking home from his New York City law office with William Sulzer, a young lawyer, on March 12, the day of the infamous blizzard of 1888. Wisely deciding to give up fighting the storm, Sulzer took a room in a hotel, but Conkling refused to surrender in the face of the fierce wind and flying snow. He made it back to his residence severely weakened and died about a month later.

COLLECTOR OF THE PORT OF NEW YORK

On November 21, 1871, at the urging of Conkling and his friends, President Grant appointed Chester Arthur to be collector of the Port of New York. In this position Arthur oversaw the operations of the New York Custom House. The custom house collected 75 percent of all **customs** fees, or taxes, on incoming goods to the United States, amounting to more than $100 million a year. The New York Custom House was the largest federal employer in the country, with 1,300 workers, all of them appointed under the spoils system.

Goods arrive at New York's South Street. The Custom House, which Arthur oversaw as collector, collected all fees and taxes on these goods.

The custom house was a den of corruption. Employees regularly skimmed money from customs fees for themselves. They also took a percentage of the illegal goods that were seized and the fines levied on such goods, a practice that was legal at the time. With the inclusion of these fees, Arthur's salary as collector soared to $50,000, equal to that of the president of the United States. Arthur himself was scrupulously honest. But he did nothing to stop those working under him from stealing. A fine dresser and a genial but demanding employer, Arthur earned the title the "Gentleman Boss."

The Boss was as good

An 1876 political cartoon depicts President Ulysses S. Grant burdened by the corruption that was present during his second term as president.

at fundraising as he was at administration. With Arthur's help in New York State, President Grant easily won reelection to a second term in 1872. The spoilsmen became more entrenched than ever in the federal government during Grant's second term. Despite his personal integrity, President Grant was pre-siding over one of the most corrupt administrations in American presidential history.

ELLEN LEWIS HERNDON ARTHUR

If she had lived, Ellen (Nell) Arthur would have been a graceful and admired first lady and certainly one of the prettiest. But fate never gave her the opportunity. She was born on August 30, 1837, in Culpeper Court House, Virginia, the only child of the naval officer William Lewis

Herndon. She had a gift for music and sang in the choir at Saint John's Episcopal Church on Washington, D.C.'s, Lafayette Square, where the family had moved. In 1856 they moved again, this time to New York City, where her father took command of a mail steamer. She was introduced to Chester Arthur by a cousin who roomed in the same boardinghouse as Arthur.

The war years were difficult ones for Ellen. She missed her relatives in Virginia, who had remained loyal to the Confederacy. Because she was a Southerner, her husband's family and friends distrusted her and questioned her loyalty to the Union. When the Arthurs moved to a fine house on Manhattan's Lexington Avenue, Ellen devoted herself to charity work and social causes until her untimely death.

Chester Arthur mourned the loss of his wife for the rest of his life. As president, he commissioned in her memory a stained glass window in Saint John's Church. From the White House he often viewed the window, illuminated by the church lights, and thought of his dear Nell.

Arthur never regained consciousness. She died on January 12; she was forty-two years old.

Chester Arthur was a broken man, wracked by grief and guilt. Great events would soon thrust him into the national spotlight and change the course of his life. But without his wife by his side, things would never be the same. As he later told a friend, "Honors to me now are not what they once were."

At the June 1880 Republican Convention in Chicago, James Garfield was nominated for president and Chester Arthur for vice president.

AN UNLIKELY VICE PRESIDENT

*R*epublican delegates from across the country flocked to their national convention in Chicago's Exposition Hall in June 1880. As the party prepared to choose a candidate in the coming general election, it was clear the Stalwarts and the Half-Breeds were heading for a showdown. President Hayes was not seeking a second term. He had pledged in his inaugural address to serve only four years and intended to keep his word. Conkling and his fellow Stalwarts were working furiously to return former president Ulysses S. Grant to the White House for an unprecedented third term. They believed Grant would end the reforms put in place after the Civil War. The Half-Breeds were supporting two moderate candidates, Senator James G. Blaine of Maine and Treasury Secretary John Sherman of Ohio.

A TENSE CONVENTION

On the first **ballot** at the convention Grant led with 304 votes, Blaine followed with 284, and Sherman trailed with 93. Grant was just 65 votes shy of a majority. But ballot after ballot followed, and the former president could not gain enough votes to win the nomination. While most Americans held Grant in high regard as a war hero, some Republican leaders had been appalled by the scandal and corruption that had dogged his administration and did not want to return him to the White House.

Finally, on the thirty-sixth ballot, the delegates turned to a **dark horse** candidate, the former governor and senator-elect of Ohio, James A. Garfield. Ironically, Garfield had come to the convention with no presidential aspirations and had given the nominating speech for his friend Sherman. But in many ways Garfield was an ideal candidate. A moderate, he stood in neither the Stalwart nor the Half-Breed camp. He had been a Union general in the Civil War and following that had spent eighteen years serving in the U.S. Congress. He was a spellbinding speaker who was well liked and respected.

However, the Stalwarts wanted their own man as president and were outraged by Garfield's nomination. Some even vowed not to support a ticket with Garfield on it. The party regulars had to do something to bring the Stalwarts back into the fold and avoid a split in the Republican Party. They decided to nominate a Stalwart to be vice president, to balance out the ticket. They offered the vice presidency to the New York banker Levi P. Morton. It was important to choose a New Yorker, since that state had the most electoral votes. Conkling, who staunchly opposed the Garfield ticket, advised Morton to turn down the opportunity, and he did. Then, to many people's surprise, Chester Arthur let it be known that if offered the nomination, he would accept. Key party members made him the offer. Before accepting the nomination, Arthur went to talk to his old mentor Conkling. The senator told Arthur that "you should drop it [the nomination] as you would a red hot [horse] shoe from the forge." But Arthur would not agree. "The office of the Vice-President," he told Conkling, "is a greater honor than I ever dreamed of attaining. . . . In a calmer moment you will look at this differently."

This photograph of Chester Arthur was taken around the time he was nominated for the vice presidency at the Republican Convention in Chicago.

THE GILDED AGE

In 1873 the authors Mark Twain and Charles Dudley Warner published a novel titled *The Gilded Age: A Tale of Today*. It is about a schemer, Colonel Beriah Sellers, who becomes involved in land speculation in Tennessee. The kind of corrupt behavior that Sellers hoped would win him a fortune was typical of the times. The term the "Gilded Age" came to represent the thirty-five years in American society following the

Civil War. It was an era of tremendous expansion in industry, business, and agriculture. In addition, however, there was more financial and political scandal and corruption than at any previous time in American history. Corrupt politicians were at work in the federal government during the two-term presidency of Ulysses S. Grant as well as at the local level. The most corrupt and well run urban political machine was that controlled by William Marcy "Boss" Tweed in New York City.

Clever, ruthless businessmen made great fortunes in industry and built showy mansions for themselves. Their excessive wealth was in stark contrast to the status of millions of immigrants who came to America from Europe and Asia looking for job opportunities at this time. While they usually found work, it was often guelling physical labor performed in unsafe conditions. The immigrants often ended up living in squalor in America's growing cities. The word "gilded" refers to something coated with gold. Underneath the gold coating of the Gilded Age was a society rotted through by corruption, waste, and injustice.

The liberals and moderates in the party were no happier with Arthur's acceptance than Conkling was. Based on the New Yorker's long involvement with machine politics, they considered Arthur a questionable choice at best. Charles Eliot Norton, a distinguished scholar and professor at Harvard University, called Arthur's nomination "a miserable farce." Some people were already asking if it would be possible to vote for Garfield but not for his running mate.

"It is true General Garfield, if elected, may die during his term in office," wrote E. L. Godkin in *The Nation*, "but that is too unlikely a contingency to be worth making extraordinary provisions for." In little more than a year Godkin's words would be considered chillingly prophetic.

Why did Arthur accept the nomination for the vice presidency? An astute politician, he may well have seen that time was running out for the Stalwarts and that the reformers in the Republican Party were gaining dominance. He also may have been anxious to restore his reputation, which had lost its luster when Hayes forced him out of the custom house.

THE ELECTION OF 1880

Arthur took his role as candidate as seriously as he had any other job he held in government service. As chairman of the state Republican Committee, he worked tirelessly, organizing rallies, setting up speakers for the campaign, and raising funds. He was asked to make few appearances as the vice presidential candidate, which was not unusual for the times. The **Democrats** nominated the Civil War general Winfield Scott Hancock as their presidential candidate and the former Indiana Congressman William H. English as vice president. James B. Weaver, another former Civil War general, ran for president for the Greenback Party, a third party that represented the urban working class and farmers.

During the campaign the Democrats went after Arthur with a vengeance. They not only attacked his credentials to serve as vice president, they even challenged his right to run for the office. They played up rumors that Arthur was a native of Ireland, and as a foreign-born citizen was ineligible under the Constitution to

A campaign poster announces Garfield and Arthur as the Republican Party candidates.

seek the vice presidency. When that rumor was proved untrue, they latched on to another rumor that Arthur had been born in Canada, just over the Vermont border, again making him ineligible. That rumor was never proven either.

On November 2, 1880, election day, more than 78 percent of the qualified voters nationwide turned out, the greatest percentage to date. The results were startling. Garfield and Arthur won a clear victory in the **electoral vote**, with 214 votes to Hancock and English's 155. Weaver won no electoral votes, although his

Garfield and Arthur are featured on an invitation to the inaugural reception for President Garfield.

total in the popular vote was nearly 306,000. The Republicans' margin in the popular vote, however, was razor thin. Out of a total of about 10 million ballots cast, the Republicans beat the Democrats by only about two thousand votes. It was the closest presidential election in American history.

A POWER STRUGGLE

As vice president, Chester Arthur seemed to fulfill his enemies' worst fears. He remained a partisan politician, openly campaigning

THE GREENBACK PARTY

During and immediately after the Civil War the Union issued cheaply made paper money, called greenbacks, to help meet the expenses of the war. Western farmers liked this increase in the money supply because they could then charge more for their crops and pay off their debts more easily. But after the war the government began to withdraw this paper money from circulation. The new policy benefited big businesses and creditors, who wanted a more stable currency, one backed by gold. The farmers wanted more greenbacks to keep them solvent, particularly after the economic Panic of 1873. The Greenback Party was established to this end in 1874 in Indianapolis, Indiana. Two years later the party nominated the inventor and philanthropist Peter Cooper for president. Cooper garnered few votes in the 1876 election, but two years later fourteen Greenback candidates were elected to Congress. The party fared less well in the 1880 election against Garfield and Arthur. The Greenback Party had a presidential candidate in the 1884 elections, but he did not do well. Not long after that the party dissolved. However, a number of the progressive issues the Greenbackers had supported in their 1880 platform later were adopted by the two major parties. They included a national income tax, an eight-hour workday, and suffrage for women. Many members of the Greenback Party later joined the more influential Populist Party.

for Stalwart candidates promoted by Conkling, with whom he was once again on good terms. Arthur hardly knew Garfield before being chosen for the ticket, and the two were not friends. Instead of supporting Garfield's appointments in New York State, Arthur regularly took Conkling's side in opposing them. Garfield was the president, however, and when he appointed James G. Blaine secretary of state in May 1881, Conkling was so furious over the election of his political nemesis that he resigned his Senate seat in protest. Thomas C. Platt, the other senator from New York, resigned as well.

But Conkling's departure did not end the new president's troubles. Every day he was beleaguered by persistent office seekers, who lined up to see him in the White House, hoping for a government appointment. This was a ritual every president in those times had to endure. Among the throngs of office seekers was a third-rate lawyer and self-promoter named Charles J. Guiteau, who had supported the Garfield-Arthur ticket and now expected to be rewarded by the winning team with a job. He pestered Garfield for the ambassadorship to Austria. He had also pleaded his case to Grant, Secretary of State Blaine, and Vice President Arthur. Guiteau became such a nuisance that in May 1881 he was barred from the White House.

ASSASSINATION

On July 2 Garfield and his two older sons were embarking on a summer vacation to New Jersey, New York, and Massachusetts, where the president was to speak at the commencement exercises of his alma mater, Williams College. He was in the Baltimore and Potomac Railroad station, accompanied by Secretary of State

Charles Guiteau, a disappointed office seeker, fatally wounded President Garfield on July 2, 1881.

Secretary of State James Blaine assists President Garfield after Garfield was shot by Charles Guiteau.

Blaine, when Charles Guiteau walked up and fired a gun at the president at point-blank range. Garfield fell, seriously wounded, with a bullet lodged in his spine. Guiteau waited calmly until police officers surrounded him. "I did it and will go to jail for it," he told them. "I am a Stalwart and Arthur will be president."

Garfield was moved back to the White House, where his condition was grim. He was expected to die that night, but he rallied and continued to live through the hot Washington summer.

Guiteau's words spoken at the crime scene were a deep embarrassment for the vice president. Although he had no connection to Guiteau's mad act, ugly rumors spread through the capital that Conkling had engineered the shooting to get Arthur into the White House. A letter was later found in Guiteau's apartment addressed to "President Arthur." In the letter Guiteau asked Arthur to make him a member of his cabinet. Guiteau made things worse for the vice president by demanding during his long trial that Arthur, who benefited from the assassination, contribute money to the defense.

Even if Conkling and Arthur had no part in Garfield's shooting, the desperate act of an office seeker and admitted Stalwart was seen by many Americans as bitter fruit of the spoils system. The public demanded a reformed civil service system, and the Republicans were put on notice.

"THE LAST MAN"

On September 6 doctors agreed to Garfield's request that he be moved to the New Jersey seashore, where fresh air and a change of scenery might improve his health. He rallied briefly and then rapidly declined, dying at 10:35 PM on September 19, 1881. Garfield had been president for only six months. A distraught Arthur took the presidential oath three hours later in the parlor of his Manhattan townhouse before the New York Supreme Court justice John R. Brady, who was summoned by messengers. Two days later Arthur repeated the oath in the

WIDOWERS IN THE WHITE HOUSE

When he became president, Chester Arthur was the fourth widower to occupy the White House. The others were Thomas Jefferson, Andrew Jackson, and Martin Van Buren. Martha Jefferson had been dead nineteen and a half years when her husband became president. Jefferson's daughter, also name Martha, occasionally served as hostess of the White House during his presidency. Dolley Madison, the popular wife of Jefferson's secretary of state James Madison, more frequently filled that role. Rachel Jackson died of a heart attack several months before she and the president-elect were scheduled to move to Washington. Jackson's niece Emily Donelson served as White House hostess. Hannah Van Buren died in 1819, while her husband was the attorney general of New York. As president, Van Buren lived with his four sons in the White House. His eldest son married during that time, and the younger Mrs. Van Buren, Angelica, served as the administration's hostess. Grover Cleveland, who would become Arthur's successor, entered the White House a bachelor and left it a married man. He married twenty-one-year-old Frances Folsom in 1886. No other president before or since has married while in the White House.

vice president's Capitol office, with former presidents Grant and Hayes looking on.

The feelings of many members of both political parties were well summed up by one Republican who exclaimed, "Chet Arthur? President of the United States? Good God!" Even *The New York*

Times, a newspaper that had praised Arthur in the past, was not impressed: "Arthur is about the last man who would be considered eligible to that position did the choice depend on the voice either of a majority of his own party or of a majority of the people of the United States," the paper wrote. Would Arthur be as partisan and divisive a figure as president as he had been as vice president? The nation held its breath and waited.

HARPER'S WEEKLY

JOURNAL OF CIVILIZATION.

VOL. XXX.—No. 1562.
Copyright, 1886, by HARPER & BROTHERS.

NEW YORK, SATURDAY, NOVEMBER 27, 1886.

TEN
WITH

Harper's Weekly *honors President Arthur on its cover in November 1886.*

CHESTER ALAN ARTHUR.—PHOTOGRAPHED BY C. M. BELL, WASHINGTON.—[SEE PAGE 767.]

A Surprising Presidency

---

*A*ll the noble aspirations of my lamented predecessor . . . to contain abuses, to enforce economy, to advance prosperity, and to promote the general welfare . . . will be garnered [gathered] in the hearts of the people," declared President Arthur in his inaugural speech, "and it will be my earnest endeavor to profit . . . by his example and experience."

The assembled guests may have thought the new president was just saying what the public wanted to hear and had no real intention of carrying out Garfield's policies. But they would be proven wrong. Arthur meant what he said. And it would not take long for Roscoe Conkling and the Stalwarts to find that out. Whether because of the sobering shock of Garfield's assassination or a deeper wish to rise to the greatness of the responsibility that had been thrust upon him, the presidency changed Arthur.

His Own Man

Few of the men in the Garfield administration believed that Arthur would follow his predecessor's moderate policies and drive for reform. "The new administration will be the center for every element of corruption, south and north," said the historian Henry Adams. "The outlook is very discouraging." Fearing the worst, three members of Garfield's cabinet—Treasury Secretary William Windom, Attorney General Wayne MacVeagh, and

Secretary of State Blaine—all resigned by December 1881. Conkling expected Arthur to appoint him to replace Blaine as secretary of state, but Arthur knew that with Conkling in his cabinet, it would appear that the Stalwart machine "Lord Roscoe" ran was in control of the administration. Instead, Arthur offered his old mentor a seat on the Supreme Court as a consolation prize. His pride hurt, Conkling turned it down. The men's relationship would never be the same again.

Although Arthur ended up appointing mostly Stalwarts to serve in the cabinet, he chose experienced and able men who were not part of Conkling's political machine. These included the New Jersey senator Frederick Frelinghuysen, who became secretary of state; Benjamin Brewster of Pennsylvania, who was appointed attorney general; and Charles Folger of New York, named secretary of the treasury. The only member of Garfield's cabinet to stay on was the secretary of war, Robert Todd Lincoln, Abraham Lincoln's only surviving child.

AN ASSASSIN'S TRIAL

Charles Guiteau, Garfield's assassin, went on trial on November 14, 1881. Guiteau was represented in court by his brother-in-law George Scoville, a lawyer who had no experience in criminal practice. The accused pleaded continually with Scoville to arrange a meeting with Arthur. In one note he wrote, "See him [the president] at once and get what time we want. He is bound to help me, and he will help me if you stick to him."

Guiteau defended himself for much of the trial, turning it into a circus with his rants. On January 14, 1882, he wrote Arthur, asking the president to speak to the prosecuting attorney

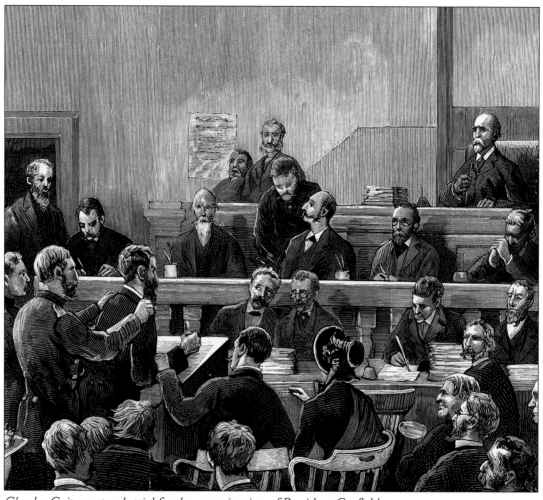

Charles Guiteau stands trial for the assassination of President Garfield.

so he "will let me down easily & the country will be satisfied with a verdict of acquittal."

About a week later Guiteau was found guilty by the jury and sentenced to death by hanging. Doctors pleaded with Arthur to order a stay of execution, believing Guiteau to be insane. But the

The Nicaragua Canal

When Chester Arthur came to the presidency, the United States had been considering the idea of digging a canal through Nicaragua for more than half a century. Secretary of State Frelinghuysen negotiated a treaty with Nicaragua whereby the Central American country would cede a piece of land to the United States for the construction of a canal that would allow ships to pass between the Atlantic and Pacific oceans without having to sail all the way around South America. Congress failed to ratify the treaty because some members believed it violated an existing treaty between the United States and Great Britain. The U.S. treaty with Nicaragua declared that neither nation would take exclusive control of a canal built on the isthmus that lay in Nicaragua. The treaty was abandoned, and the Nicaragua Canal was never built. Another canal, through Panama, was proposed during the administration of President Theodore Roosevelt. Work began in May 1904 and was completed ten years later.

Secretary of State Frelinghuysen's treaties with Mexico and Santo Domingo (now the Dominican Republic) were also opposed by Congress and special interest groups that wanted to keep economic control of Latin America in U.S. hands.

plea of insanity that exists in the judicial system today was not then available, and on the advice of his attorney general, Arthur refused to authorize a stay of execution. "It will shake the public confidence in the certainty and justice of the courts, by substituting your will for the judgment of law," Brewster wrote. Guiteau was executed on June 30.

THE STAR ROUTE FRAUDS

Before he was shot, Garfield had ordered the postmaster general to look into an alleged fraud case: members of the postmaster general's staff were said to be using federal funds to contract private companies to deliver mail to remote parts of the West. Some of these routes were rumored not to exist, theoretically allowing the staff members to pocket millions of dollars allocated for the phony contracts. The case came to be called the Star Route frauds after the star, or asterisk, stamped on the documents. The Stalwarts urged Arthur to drop the case, but he called for the investigation to go forward. Two Stalwarts, Stephen Dorsey and Thomas Brady, were accused of skimming. Arthur surprised both his friends and enemies by calling for the full prosecution of these two men and seven others. After a three-month trial, in June 1882 Dorsey and most of his codefendants were acquitted. Jury tampering was uncovered, but a second trial failed to end in convictions as well.

THE CIVIL SERVICE PRESIDENT

In his first annual message to Congress, delivered on December 6, 1881, Arthur put forth a set of goals for his presidency. He called for an increase in volunteers in the army to help protect settlers in the West from American Indians. At the same time he proposed that Indian reservation lands be protected from settlers and that a plan to help Indians achieve full citizenship be established. He also

Berhard Gillam satirizes the Star Route frauds, led by Stalwarts Stephen Dorsey and Thomas Brady.

called for the setting up of a government for the new U.S. territory of Alaska and for the construction of a building to house the Library of Congress in Washington. But he devoted the greatest part of his address to civil service reform, the major goal of his predecessor. While acknowledging the need for reform, Arthur

George H. Pendleton

Senator George Pendleton experienced as many ups and downs as any American politician of his day. Born in Cincinnati, Ohio, in 1825, he began his career as many aspiring politicians did, as an attorney. He was elected to the U.S. Congress in 1857 and was reelected three times. Strongly opposed to the Union's involvement in the Civil War, Pendleton ran for vice president on the Democratic ticket in 1864. He

and the presidential candidate George B. McClellan lost to Abraham Lincoln and Andrew Johnson. In 1869 Pendleton ran for governor of Ohio and lost to the Republican Rutherford B. Hayes, who would go on to become president. After working for ten years as a railroad executive, Pendleton was elected to the U.S. Senate. During his sole term in the Senate he sponsored the bill that bears his name. Pendleton, who left the Senate in 1885, served as an envoy to Germany until his death, in 1889.

advised Congress to proceed slowly. "The evils which are complained of cannot be eradicated at once; the work must be gradual," he said.

The Democratic senator George Pendleton of Ohio had introduced a bill calling for major changes in the federal civil service program back in December 1880. The bill languished until the assassination of Garfield. "[The] crime acted on public opinion very like a spark on a powder-magazine," wrote one newspaper editorial writer, "[and set off a] mass of popular indignation all ready to explode." The Pendleton Bill would require that most potential federal employees be evaluated on a merit system, effectively ending the spoils system. It would establish an agency, the U.S. Civil Service Commission, that would oversee all federal hiring and would require some jobs to be filled on the basis of competitive exams. Arthur strongly supported the Pendleton Civil Service Act, but most Republicans opposed it, and it stalled in Senate committees for more than a year.

THE CHINESE EXCLUSION ACT

The president found himself at odds with Congress on two other major pieces of legislation. In 1882 a Republican senator, John Miller of California, drew up a bill that would keep Chinese immigrants from entering the United States for twenty years. The immigration bill also denied citizenship to all Chinese immigrants already living in the country. The bill reflected the growing prejudice of many Americans, especially those in California, where most of the Chinese immigrants resided. Religious groups claimed the Chinese were "anti-Christian." Other people complained unfairly that they were unclean and prone to criminal activity. Still others, who claimed to have scientific evidence, declared that Asians were

A political cartoon depicts a Chinese immigrant barred from entry to the United States as a result of the Chinese Exclusion Act.

physically and mentally inferior to white Americans. All these claims were groundless. Nevertheless, Congress passed the bill, and it went to the president for his consideration.

Arthur, who had shown his sympathy for minorities through his long stand against slavery, felt it was wrong to deny citizenship

THE CHINESE IN AMERICA

The anti-Chinese feeling that fueled the passage of the Chinese Exclusion Act was in sharp contrast to attitudes toward the Chinese that was a generation earlier. After the Civil War the nation grew quickly, and there was a great demand for labor in industry and railroad construction. Immigrants from China and elsewhere filled that demand. The Burlingame Treaty of 1868 between the United States and China provided for unlimited Chinese immigration to America. Chinese labor helped build the Transcontinental Railroad, which was completed in 1869.

(continued)

After the completion of the major railroad lines, Chinese immigrants turned to other occupations. They opened laundries and restaurants. They worked in mines, in factories, and on farms. By 1882 there were 250,000 Chinese living in the United States. Because the Chinese were willing to work for lower wages than American-born workers would accept, fears of job loss were prevalent. In 1880 China conceded the right of the United States to limit Chinese immigration but not stop it completely. However, two years later, that was exactly what Congress decided to do.

The total exclusion of Chinese immigrants did not end until 1943, when China became an ally of the United States during World War II. That year President Franklin D. Roosevelt set up a quota system allowing 105 Chinese to immigrate to the United States each year. This system was in place until 1965.

to Chinese Americans. He also said the bill violated existing treaties with China and would deal a devastating blow to the American economy. It would, he said, "repel Oriental nations from us and . . . drive their trade and commerce into more friendly hands." For these reasons he vetoed the bill when it arrived on his desk.

Liberals across the country praised Arthur's action. Many other Americans, particularly those living in the West, hated him for it. In California and other western states the president was burned in **effigy**. Congress revised the anti-immigration bill, reducing the twenty-year exclusion to ten years, but otherwise kept it intact.

Both congressional houses passed the revised bill, thus overriding the president's veto. Arthur reluctantly signed the bill into law. The Chinese Exclusion Act would be renewed in 1892 and 1902.

THE RIVERS AND HARBORS BILL

The second major struggle between Congress and President Arthur was over money. In 1882 Congress approved $19 million to be used for the improvement of rivers and harbors. While the Rivers and Harbors Bill had some merit, Arthur believed that the amount of money allocated for the project was too large. The bill targeted the Potomac River, which passes through Washington, D.C., and the Mississippi River. Money would be used to drain many of the marshes that lined the Potomac and to make the Mississippi more navigable. But other proposals in the bill were for more local projects that would not benefit interstate trade or transportation. This was **pork barrel** legislation—the congressmen would use the money to reward local businessmen for their support on election day and pocket some of the remaining funds for themselves. From his years in the custom house Arthur realized all too well how easy it was for politicians to skim federal money for themselves. He used his veto, but again Congress overrode it, and the bill passed.

One reason why there was so much money available in the U.S. Treasury for Congress to spend was that the Treasury had an annual surplus of $80 million to $100 million. The money mostly came from the collection of the high **tariffs** and taxes imposed on imported goods. Arthur and other government officials wanted to see the tariffs reduced and the surplus money circulated back into the economy, where it could benefit the average American.

President Arthur was known for his elegant dress and social graces.

Or, as another disappointed Republican crony put it, "He isn't Chet Arthur any more—he's the President."

FATHER OF THE STEEL NAVY

Aside from the issue of civil service reform, President Arthur found himself more at odds than in agreement with the Democrat-controlled Congress during the second half of his term. However, he had considerable success in one area.

In the twenty years since the end of the Civil War, the U.S. Navy had fallen into a state of shameful disarray. It was, in the words of *The Nation*, "a satirical semblance of a navy." Nearly every nation of Europe and some in Latin America had far stronger navies. One of the problems was that American naval ships were made of wood, which had deteriorated over the years. About 90 percent of these wooden ships were gone by Arthur's presidency.

From the start of his presidency Arthur took a strong interest in improving the navy. He supported Secretary of the Navy William E. Chandler's proposal for the construction of four new ships made of steel—three cruisers and a dispatch boat. After some foot-dragging, Congress finally came through with the **appropriations** in 1883. Other obstacles, including accidental fires and shoddy materials, slowed progress. Only one of the ships was completed by the end of Arthur's term. When they finally were all in service, the ships were widely admired as the most seaworthy of all U.S. naval vessels.

Secretary of the Navy Chandler also helped found the Naval War College in Newport, Rhode Island, and the Office of Naval Intelligence in Washington, D.C. The U.S. Navy

The USS Petrel *was one of the first ships completed during the rebuilding of the United States' naval fleet.*

would continue to grow and modernize for the next decade and a half, helping America win a sweeping victory in the Spanish-American War, which was fought in Cuba and the Philippines in 1898. For these achievements Chester Arthur is justly called the Father of the Steel Navy.

THE DUDE PRESIDENT

If President Arthur's power was restricted by Congress in national politics, his influence reigned supreme in the social whirl of Washington, D.C. No president has been better dressed or more socially adept.

The president's reputation as "Elegant Arthur" or "the Dude President" was well earned. He chose his clothes with

This 1884 political cartoon, titled "The Progress of Snobbery," satirizes President Arthur's love of luxury and refinement.

the seriousness of a fashion plate. The president was rumored to own eighty pairs of pants, and he bought suits by the dozen from his New York tailor. He favored tuxedos at White House dinners and had his valet regularly trim his long sideburns. He brought his personal cook with him to the White House and hired a French chef from New York to take charge of the menus of the fifty state dinners held during his term.

President Arthur loved to entertain and did so with great style. According to one White House worker, "He wanted the best of everything, and wanted it served in the best manner." Not everyone approved of Arthur's lavish parties and entertainments. Former president Hayes, who had banned alcohol from the White House, complained, "Nothing like it ever before in the Executive Mansion—liquor, snobbery, and worse." With no spouse to fill the role of White House hostess, Arthur persuaded his younger sister, forty-year-old Mary McElroy, to move in and take on that important position. She did so with a charm and style that matched his own.

REDECORATING THE WHITE HOUSE

As soon as he became president, Arthur went to work renovating the stuffy, worn-out White House. He had twenty-four wagonloads of old furniture and many antiques, some dating as far back as the administration of John Adams, carted away and sold at public auction. He hired the thirty-three-year-old designer Louis Tiffany to redecorate the president's mansion. Nearly every evening Arthur, who spent his first three months in office living in other quarters, would drop in to inspect the work and make suggestions. By the time he moved in, in December 1881,

Mary McElroy, "First Sister"

Although she was never an official first lady, Arthur's sister, whom he called Molly, did as good a job as White House hostess as any president's wife. She spent each fall through spring living at the White House with her two daughters, May and Jessie, while her understanding husband, who sold insurance, stayed home in Albany, New York, with their two sons. The family reunited in the summer. As the unofficial hostess, Molly enjoyed a greater sense of independence than any first

lady had. While an unspoken law prevented presidents' wives from being seen in public restaurants and at the homes of private citizens, Molly was free to visit her friends and loved going out. At the White House she regularly presided over fourteen-course state dinners, where the wine flowed freely and the conversation was carefree. All this gaiety undoubtedly took her brother's mind off the sad fact that his late beloved wife would never know the pleasures of being hostess at the White House.

Louis Comfort Tiffany

Louis Tiffany, the most influential American decorative designer of the late nineteenth and early twentieth centuries, was born in 1848, the eldest son of jeweler and businessman Charles Lewis Tiffany. At age eighteen, against his father's wishes, Louis decided on a career as an artist. He became a respected painter of watercolor landscapes, but in 1875 he turned his energies to what he termed "decorative work" and three years later opened a glass factory. Tiffany used his unique

colored glass to make everything from lamp shades to vases to cigarette boxes. By 1898 his factories were churning out five thousand different colors and varieties of glass.

Tiffany never lost his interest in fine art and began a foundation for struggling artists at his home on Long Island, New York. He died in 1933. "I have always striven to fix beauty in wood or stone or glass or pottery, in oil or water color by using whatever seemed fittest for the expression of beauty" he once wrote.

the White House was a showcase of Victorian style. Further redecorating took place in the autumn of 1882. The walls of public rooms shimmered with gold leaf. There was an elevator to take visitors upstairs—the first to be installed in the White House. Tiffany built a 50-foot-long screen of jeweled glass to separate the main corridor of the mansion from the north hallway. The total cost of the renovations was more than $30,000—in today's money, about $2 million.

A President's Pastimes

Arthur was not known to be an industrious worker. He often began work after 10 AM and quit by 4 PM. "President Arthur never did today what he could put off until tomorrow," said a White House clerk years later. He would take a daily walk or ride in his fashionable dark green carriage, its interior lined with morocco leather and cloth; a lap robe made of Labrador otter protected the president from winter chills. "It is no exaggeration to say that it [the presidential carriage] is the finest which has ever appeared in the streets of the capital," gushed *The New York Times*. When he went strolling on the boulevards of Washington, Arthur always wore a fresh flower in his buttonhole and had a kind and genial word for every passerby. "It is not that he is handsome and agreeable—for he was both long ago," noted one admirer, "but it is his ease, polish and perfect manner that makes him the greatest society lion we have had in many years."

He dined punctiliously at seven with his children and sister unless he was entertaining guests or presiding over a state dinner. Late at night he'd curl up with a good book. The English novelists

YELLOWSTONE, THE FIRST NATIONAL PARK

The first white man to see the Yellowstone region and its many natural wonders was probably the mountain man and trapper John Colter. He crossed the area on foot in 1807 and 1808. Over the next several decades scores of mountain men visited Yellowstone, but few believed their stories of its gushing geysers and bubbling potholes. Finally, in 1870 a government survey team visited the region and confirmed the reports. Two years later Congress passed a bill to establish Yellowstone as the first national park, to be protected and enjoyed by all Americans. By the time Arthur visited Yellowstone, it was a mecca for tourists. However, problems with hunters and trappers in the park persisted until the army took over in 1886. A detachment of the U.S. Cavalry kept order in Yellowstone until 1916, when Congress established the National Parks Service to oversee the park and nine subsequently created national parks.

Charles Dickens and William Makepeace Thackery were his favorite authors. Arthur rarely went to bed before 2 AM.

Arthur was an avid fisherman and enjoyed horseback riding. He liked to travel around the country. Because the nation was relatively prosperous and at peace during his term, he had plenty of opportunities to fish, ride, and be a tourist. His longest and most controversial presidential trip was to the newly named Yellowstone National Park, in Wyoming and Montana, in August 1883.

When not running the country, President Arthur (far left) enjoyed fishing.

His entourage, led by the Civil War hero Philip Sheridan, included family members, military officers, American-Indian guides, and 175 pack animals. The Democrats in Congress roundly criticized the expense of this "inspection" at the public's expense. Arthur responded in a huff, telling a reporter, "They speak of my journeys as junketings. I need a holiday as much as the poorest of my fellow citizens."

On another occasion, while he was traveling along the coast, news spread that Arthur was seriously ill. He vehemently denied it, saying, "I am feeling perfectly well. I have not been sick at all."

In fact the president was indeed ill, very ill, but he chose to keep it a secret from nearly everyone.

Courageous to the Last

*S*ome time during his term as president, probably in 1882, Arthur learned that he had Bright's disease, a serious kidney ailment. At the time the illness was considered incurable. The president of the United States knew he was slowly dying. Yet he had no intention of leaving the White House as an invalid, with people pitying him. He kept the news of his disease a secret from even his closest friends. The only person he informed was his son Alan.

The Election of 1884

Recognizing that it would seem odd if he did not seek reelection when his term ended, Arthur made a half-hearted effort to run for his party's nomination in 1884. The truth was, even if he had been healthy enough to survive a second term, Arthur's chances of winning the nomination were slim. His former friends among the Stalwarts felt betrayed because of his support of civil service reform. The more moderate wing of the party, for its part, had never fully trusted Arthur because of his Stalwart past. The former team player and party loyalist found himself abandoned—a president without a party.

Nevertheless, he had enough support at the Republican Convention in June 1884 to garner 278 votes on the first ballot. James G. Blaine, Arthur's former secretary of state and his principal rival for the nomination, received 334.5 votes. By the fourth

Delegates cheer the nomination of James Blaine as the presidential candidate at the 1884 Republican Convention in Chicago.

BRIGHT'S DISEASE

Bright's disease was named after Richard Bright, the English physician who first described its symptoms in 1827. The disease is characterized by a severe inflammation of the kidneys that reduces the production of urine, which then accumulates in the body. The face or even the entire body may take on a puffy appearance. Those afflicted with it suffer from feelings of inertia and depression. Today, medications and, if need be, dialysis treatment, can control the effects of the disease, now called acute nephritis. In Arthur's day, however, Bright's disease was an almost certain death sentence.

Among other famous people who died from Bright's disease are the first wives of presidents Teddy Roosevelt and Woodrow Wilson, as well as the Scottish-Canadian explorer Sir Alexander Mackenzie, the horror writer H. P. Lovecraft, and the movie character actor Sydney Greenstreet. Perhaps the most famous person to die of the disease was the poet Emily Dickinson, who succumbed six months before President Arthur did.

ballot Arthur's support had dropped to 207 votes, and Blaine had 541 votes, enough to clinch the nomination. In the general election in November Blaine lost in a close race to the Democrat Grover Cleveland, who by then had left the Buffalo mayoralty behind and become governor of New York. Blaine has the dubious distinction of being the only **nonincumbent** Republican candidate to lose a presidential race between 1860 and 1912.

James G. Blaine, Perennial Presidential Hopeful

When James Blaine received the presidential nomination of his party in 1884, it was the fulfillment of a lifelong dream. Twice before, in 1876 and 1880, Blaine had tried for the

nomination, and both times he had failed. The failure was partly his own doing. Blaine had served as Speaker of the House of Representatives from 1869 to 1875. During that time he had done legislative favors for railroad companies in exchange for gifts of railroad stock. James Mulligan, a clerk in Boston, possessed and revealed incriminating letters exposing Blaine's misuse of power. The subsequent scandal contributed both to Blaine's nomination losses and to his failure to win the presidency.

In the 1888 election Blaine supported the Republican candidate Benjamin Harrison for president. When Harrison won, he made Blaine his secretary of state, the position Blaine had held under Garfield. As secretary of state Blaine made a major contribution to U.S.–Latin American relations and supported the first Pan-American Conference, held in Washington, D.C., in 1889–1890. But Blaine still yearned to be president. He tried once more for the nomination of his party in 1892 and failed. He died the following year.

LAST ACTS IN OFFICE

One of Chester Arthur's last acts as president was to preside over the dedication of the Washington Monument on February 21, 1885, the day before George Washington's birthday. On his next-to-last day in office, Arthur asked the Senate to reinstate his old political ally, Ulysses S. Grant, onto the lists of retired Civil War officers, giving him full pay as a general. Grant had fallen on hard times, was dying of cancer, and could not provide for his family. It was an act of great kindness. The former president died on July 23, 1885.

FINAL DAYS

Before leaving the White House after Cleveland's inauguration, the presidential adviser George Bliss asked Arthur what his future plans were. "Well," he replied, "there doesn't seem to be anything

THE WASHINGTON MONUMENT

Few landmarks in the nation's capital were as long in the making as the Washington Monument. In 1783 Congress approved the construction of a statue of George Washington, but Washington objected. A memorial to our first president was pursued by the private Washington National Monument Society in 1832. The design, created by the architect Robert Mills, included a tall obelisk composed of marble, granite, and sandstone, surrounded by a huge Greek-style temple (right). The temple was never built. Work on the obelisk began in 1848 and took forty years to complete. The long delay was due to a lack of funds and the disruption caused by the Civil War. Congress took over the project in 1876 and appropriated money to continue construction. When completed, the Washington Monument stood 555 feet 3 inches tall and weighed 91,000 tons. Because of the need to apply finishing touches, the monument dedicated by Arthur in 1885 was not opened to the public until October 1888. At that time the Washington Monument was the world's tallest structure. It held that position until the completion of the Eiffel Tower a year later. Today, the monument remains the world's tallest obelisk and the tallest structure in Washington, D.C. More than 800,000 people visit it each year, riding up an elevator in its hollow interior to gain a magnificent view of the capital and parts of neighboring Maryland and Virginia.

else for an ex-President to do but to go into the country and raise big pumpkins."

But Arthur was a city man, and he returned to New York City and his townhouse on Lexington Avenue. He went back to his law practice briefly but found he did not have the strength for it. Friends urged him to run for a seat in the U.S. Senate, but he refused. He did accept the presidency of the New York Arcade Railway Company, which was planning to build a subway system in New York City. In February 1886 a medical exam showed that Bright's disease had caused a serious heart condition, and Arthur retired from the railway company. He spent most of his remaining days at home, in the company of his two children and other relatives. Alan Arthur had graduated from Princeton University the previous spring. During this time the former president asked an old friend from his custom house days to destroy all his personal and official papers.

On the morning of November 17, 1886, Arthur suffered a massive cerebral hemorrhage. He died the following day, at 5 AM, with his children by his side. He was fifty-seven years old and had left the presidency just twenty months earlier. "He died as he lived, a gentleman," a friend said. His private physician described him as "a brave, strong man to the last, and few men deserved better to live." Chester Arthur was buried alongside his wife and firstborn son in Albany, New York, on a ridge overlooking the Hudson River valley.

Legacy

Chester Arthur will never be considered a great president. But then neither will any of the men who served in the White House between the administrations of Abraham Lincoln and Theodore Roosevelt. This period of American history was a time of great growth and development. It was a time of relative peace and prosperity. There were few real crises that required a strong leader, and Americans were happy to have a president who did not take a very active role in running the nation's affairs. That was left largely to Congress, which during these years held more power than the president and prevented him from dominating the government.

But among these less than distinguished presidents, Chester Arthur stands out, along with Rutherford B. Hayes, Grover Cleveland, and William McKinley, as among the best. Like Hayes, he was decent, good, and honest, and an adept administrator. Although his will was thwarted time and time again by Congress, Arthur stood up for what he believed in, opposing immigration exclusion, high tariffs, and pork barrel legislation. He helped foster the modern American navy, which grew larger and more impressive under each succeeding president's administration. Yet his greatest legacy may well be his support and promotion of civil service reform, which was the beginning of the end of the corrupt spoils system in national government. In so doing Arthur sacrificed his future in politics, turning on the very men who had been his colleagues and supporters.

Perhaps no person came to the presidency with lower public expectations and then so far exceeded them. And if a person's life can be summed up by the way he or she faces death, then Chester Arthur led a life of courage, strength, and dignity. "I am but one in the 55,000,000," said the author Mark Twain, who was known to have little love for politicians. "Still, in the opinion of this one-fifty-five millionth of the country's population, it would be hard to better President Arthur's administration."

In 1899 a bronze statue of Arthur was dedicated in Madison Square, just a few blocks from his longtime residence on Lexington Avenue. In his dedication speech the distinguished statesman and future secretary of war Elihu Root recalled Arthur's difficulties following Garfield's death: "Surely no more lonely and pathetic figure was ever seen assuming the powers of government." Root went on to observe how Arthur surmounted these obstacles to become a worthy president. "He was wise in statesmanship and firm and effective in administration. . . . Good causes found in him a friend and bad measures met in him an unyielding opponent."

Although his administration took place during a time of peace and growth in U.S. history, Chester Arthur is regarded as one of the best administrators to hold the office of president of the United States.

1829
Born October 5 in Fairfield, Vermont

1848
Graduates from Union College

1854
Admitted to the bar to practice law

1859
Marries Ellen (Nell) Herndon

1862
Appointed quartermaster general of New York State during the Civil War

1800

1871
Appointed Collector of the Custom House of the Port of New York

1880
Elected to the vice presidency

1881
Assumes the presidency on the death of President James Garfield

1883
Signs the Pendleton Civil Service Act into law

1886
Dies in New York City on November 18

1890

NOTES

CHAPTER 1

p. 7, "Arthur will be President." Zachary Karabell, *Chester Alan Arthur*. New York: Holt, Rinehart & Winston, 2004, p. 59.

p.8, "I dare not disturb him . . ." Thomas Reeves, *Gentleman Boss: The Life of Chester Alan Arthur*. Newtown, CT: American Political Biography Press, 2002, p. 247.

p. 11, "Reverend William Arthur was . . ." Reeves, *Gentleman Boss*, p. 6.

p. 11, "His eyes were dark . . ." Reeves, *Gentleman Boss*, p. 8.

p. 12, "I have been in many a political battle . . ." Reeves, *Gentleman Boss*, p. 17.

p. 12, "In disposition he was . . ." Reeves, *Gentleman Boss*, p. 18.

p. 19, ". . . colored persons, if sober . . ." Reeves, *Gentleman Boss*, p. 16.

CHAPTER 2

p. 29, ". . . industrious, energetic . . . official duties." Reeves, *Gentleman Boss*, p. 24.

p. 31, "[H]is practical good sense . . ." Reeves, *Gentleman Boss*, p. 30.

p. 31, "We have lost our darling boy . . ." Reeves, *Gentleman Boss*, p. 35.

p. 33, "We are told that . . ." Karabell, *Chester Alan Arthur*, p. 20.

p. 38, ". . . the snivel service." Reeves, *Gentleman Boss*, p. 59.

p. 38, "[T]he condition of the civil service . . ." Reeves, *Gentleman Boss*, p. 63.

p. 41, "Honors to me now are . . ." Reeves, *Gentleman Boss*, p. 59.

CHAPTER 3

p. 44, "You should drop it . . ." Reeves, *Gentleman Boss*, p. 80.

p. 44, "The office of the Vice President . . ." Reeves, *Gentleman Boss*, p. 57.

p. 47, ". . . a miserable farce." Karabell, *Chester Alan Arthur*, p. 42.

p. 48, "It is true General Garfield, if elected . . ." Reeves, *Gentleman Boss*, p. 60.

p. 54, "I did it and will go . . ." Karabell, *Chester Alan Arthur*, p. 59.

p. 56, "Chet Arthur? President of the United States? Good God!" Karabell, *Chester Alan Arthur*, p. 1.

p. 57, "Arthur is about the last man . . ." Karabell, *Chester Alan Arthur*, p. 63.

CHAPTER 4

p. 59, "All the noble aspirations . . ." Reeves, *Gentleman Boss*, p. 248.

p. 59, "The new administration will be . . ." Karabell, *Chester Alan Arthur*, pp. 69–70.

p. 60, "See him at once . . ." Reeves, *Gentleman Boss*, p. 263.

p. 62, "Will let me down . . ." Reeves, *Gentleman Boss*, p. 263.

p. 65, "It will shake the public . . ." Reeves, *Gentleman Boss*, p. 264.

p. 67, "The evils which are complained . . ." Reeves, *Gentleman Boss*, p. 266.

p. 67, "[The] crime acted on public opinion . . ." Bernard Weisberger, "Reinventing Government, 1882," *American Heritage*, February/March 1994, p. 22.

p. 70, ". . . repel Oriental nations from us . . ." Karabell, *Chester Alan Arthur*, p. 85.

p. 72, "President Arthur was the worst . . ." Karabell, *Chester Alan Arthur*, p. 101.

CHAPTER 5

p. 73, "I have but one annoyance . . . .", Reeves, *Gentleman Boss*, p. 354.

p. 75, "He isn't Chet Arthur . . . .", Reeves, *Gentleman Boss*, p. 86.

p. 75, "a satirical semblance of a navy" Karabell, *Chester Alan Arthur*, p. 117.

p. 78, "He wanted the best . . ." Reeves, *Gentleman Boss*, p. 270.

p. 78, "Nothing like it ever before . . ." Reeves, *Gentleman Boss*, p. 271.

p. 80, "I have always striven to fix . . ." "The Unexpected Art of Louis Comfort Tiffany," *American Heritage*, October/November 1979, p. 54.

p. 81, "President Arthur never did today . . ." Reeves, *Gentleman Boss*, p. 273.

p. 81, "It is no exaggeration to say . . ." Karabell, *Chester Alan Arthur*, p. 78.

p. 81, "It is not that he . . ." Reeves, *Gentleman Boss*, p. 272.

p. 84, "They speak of my journeys . . ." Carl Sferrazza Anthony, *America's First Families*. New York: Touchstone, 2000, p. 267.

p. 84, "I am feeling perfectly well . . ." Anthony, *America's First Families*, p. 201.

CHAPTER 6

p. 89, "Well, there doesn't seem to be anything . . ." Reeves, *Gentleman Boss*, p. 412.

p. 92, "He died as he lived, a gentleman." Karabell, *Chester Alan Arthur*, p. 138.

p. 92, "a brave, strong man . . ." Reeves, *Gentleman Boss*, p. 417.

p. 93, "I am but one in the 55,000,000 . . ." David C. Whitney, *The American Presidents*. New York: Prentice Hall, 1990, p. 179.

p. 94, "Surely no more lonely . . ." Reeves, *Gentleman Boss*, p. 419.

GLOSSARY

abolitionist a person who supported the end of slavery in the United States

Anti-Masonic Party early American third political party; existed from 1826 to about 1832

appropriations federal funds set aside for a special purpose

ballot a sheet of paper on which a vote is cast; a round of voting

bipartisan including members of both major political parties

chartered defined as official by a document

customs duties or fees imposed on imported goods

dark horse a candidate who is nominated unexpectedly at a political convention

Democrats members of one of America's two major political parties founded in 1828

depression a period of steep decline in the economy

effigy a crude representation of a person used to ridicule him or her

electoral vote the votes cast during national presidential elections by special representatives from each state

envoy a diplomatic representative ranking below an ambassador

Half-Breed a member of a group of moderate, reform-minded Republicans that formed in the late 1870s and early 1880s and who supported the candidacy of James G. Blaine in the 1880 presidential election

impeachment the act of removing a public official from office because of his or her misconduct

incumbent person holding a political office

isthmus a narrow strip of land bordered by water that connects two larger landmasses

nonincumbent a candidate for office who has not already held that office

Panic of 1873 an economic depression triggered when a Philadelphia banking house overextended itself on railroad bonds

philanthropist a person who donates money, property, or time to help those in need

popular vote the votes cast by citizens

pork barrel legislation a government bill or appropriation that funds local improvements that will not benefit the majority of people; this legislation makes constituents grateful to their legislator

quartermaster military officer in charge of obtaining quarters, food, and supplies for troops

Radical Republicans a group of Republican senators who, after the Civil War, supported strict federal control over the defeated states of the Confederacy

Reconstruction the process whereby states that had seceded were brought back into the Union after the Civil War

Republican Party one of America's two major political parties, founded in 1854

seceding breaking away or separating from, as the Southern states did from the Union before the Civil War

spoils system a political arrangement that rewards loyal party workers with paid positions in government, regardless of their qualifications

Stalwart a member of a group of conservative Republicans who supported Ulysses S. Grant for president in 1880 in hopes that he would return the spoils system of patronage to government

suffrage the right to vote

tariffs a system of duties applied by a government to import or export products

Whig Party an American political party that existed from about 1834 to 1855

Further Information

Books

Aronson, Billy. *Ulysses S. Grant* (Presidents and Their Times). New York: Marshall Cavendish Benchmark, 2008.

Elish, Dan. *Chester A. Arthur* (Encyclopedia of Presidents, Second Series). Danbury, CT: Children's Press, 2004.

Feldman, Ruth Tenzer. *Chester A. Arthur* (Presidential Leaders). Minneapolis, MN: Lerner, 2006.

Shrock, Joel. *The Gilded Age* (American Popular Culture Through History). Westport, CT: Greenwood Press, 2004.

Venezia, Mike. *Chester A. Arthur* (Getting to Know the U.S. Presidents). Danbury, CT: Children's Press, 2006.

Web Sites

American President: An Online Reference Resource

www.millercenter.virginia.edu/academic/americanpresident/arthur

This informative site includes short, concise biographies of not only Arthur but also of his wife and all the members of his cabinet.

Presidents of the United States

www.presidentsusa.net/arthur.html

This Chester Arthur home page links to many Arthur biographies, speeches, pictures, and other Web sites maintained by the U.S. government.

The White House

www.whitehouse.gov/history/presdients/ca21.html

The official White House Web site features Arthur's story as part of the ongoing tale of American presidents, from George Washington to George W. Bush.

American Presidents: Life Portraits

www.americanpresidents.org/presidents/presidents.asp?President Number=21

Portraits of each president are highlighted along with basic biographical facts, trivia, and presidential historic sites.

BIBLIOGRAPHY

American Heritage. "The Unexpected Art of Louis Comfort Tiffany." October/November, 1979, pp. 60–61.

Anthony, Carl Sferrazza. *America's First Families*. New York: Touchstone, 2000.

Beschloss, Michael, ed. *American Heritage Illustrated History of the Presidents*. New York: Crown Publishers, 2000.

Cunliffe, Marcus. *The American Heritage History of the Presidency*. New York: American Heritage Publishing, 1968.

Diller, David C. and Stephen L. Robertson. *The Presidents, First Ladies, and Vice Presidents*. Washington, D.C.: Congressional Quarterly, 1997.

Durant, John, and Alice Durant. *Pictorial History of American Presidents*. New York: A. S. Barnes, 1955.

Karabell, Zachary. *Chester Alan Arthur*. New York: Holt, Rinehart & Winston, 2004.

Reeves, Thomas C. *Gentleman Boss: The Life of Chester Alan Arthur*. Newtown, CT: American Political Biography Press, 2002. (Originally published by Alfred A. Knopf, 1975.)

Weisburger, Bernard. "Reinventing Government, 1882." American Heritage, February/March, 1994, pp. 20, 22.

Whitney, David C. *The American Presidents*. New York: Prentice Hall, 1990.

INDEX

Pages in **boldface** are illustrations.

★ ★ ★ ★ ★ ★ ★ ★ ★ ★ ★ ★ ★ ★ ★ ★ ★ ★ ★

ABOUT THE AUTHOR

Steven Otfinoski is the author of *Calvin Coolidge* in the Presidents and Their Times series. He is the author of more than twenty-five other nonfiction titles for Marshall Cavendish. Otfinoski lives in Connecticut with his wife, Beverly, an editor and high school English teacher.